ONLINE MARKETING FOR HOME INSPECTORS

INTERNET MARKETING, SEO & WEBSITE DESIGN SECRETS FOR GETTING MORE INSPECTIONS FROM THE INTERNET

CARTESS ROSS

Our Contact Details:

support@InspectMania.com
www.InspectMania.com

Limits of Liability and Disclaimer of Warranty

Warning – Disclaimer

Welcome to Inspect Mania

Welcome and thank you for downloading our free marketing guide. You've taken the very first step in growing your home inspection business.

I've had the great fortune to literally work with hundreds of home inspectors from around the world. The strategies you'll learn today will work regardless of what part of the world you're in.

I've seen firsthand, how inspectors who were only getting 1-2 inspections per week, grow to the point of conducting 40+ inspections per month. If more inspections are what you're in need of, this guide will help you get them.

I'll be honest with you though. There's a bunch of stuff I'll be covering in this manual. Trying to implement it can be over-whelming for most people. But if you take your time and pace yourself, I'm confident you'll be able to implement a bunch of this stuff yourself.

If at anytime you determine you'd rather let us implement these strategies for you, simply contact us via our website at www.InspectMania.com and we'll be glad to do it all for you.

Inspect Your Home Inspection Website's Performance. Get a FREE Local Visibility Report.

Visit our website below to get a FREE Local Visibility Report. This report will quickly show how well your home inspection business is represented on the major online directories. We invite you to run this report and see what may be preventing your inspection firm from getting more new clients.

Go to the following website now to get your FREE report:

www.InspectMania.com

CONTENTS

INTRODUCTION

Want to be the 900-pound gorilla in your local market-place? I will show you how! Many of the strategies I'll share with you will have to do with 'positioning yourself as the authority and expert'. And one way we do that is by making you show up everywhere in your local market.

Here's what we'll cover in this marketing guide of inspectors:

- **Why Internet Marketing & SEO is important for inspectors**

- **Understanding the Search Engines** (Pay-Per-Click Advertising vs. Free Organic Rankings vs. Google Map Listings)

- **How to get your inspection business on the Google Map**

  o Step-by-step guide to claiming your Google My Business listing

  o Google My Business optimization best practices

  o Our online review acquisition strategy

- **SEO Strategies for Home and Commercial Inspectors**

  o Optimizing your inspection website for the right keywords

- o My favorite link building strategies for ranking higher

- o Most commonly searched keywords for inspections

- **The most important online directories for inspectors**

- **Social Media Strategy for Home Inspectors**

- **Recap**

- **Checklist**

- **Next Steps**

WHY INTERNET MARKETING AND SEO IS IMPORTANT FOR YOUR INSPECTION BUSINESS

Most home inspectors already understand that the Internet and search engines are EXTREMELY important to the long-term growth and sustainability of their business. But occasionally I get the question, **"Why are search engines and search engine marketing so important to home inspectors?"**

Here are a couple of reasons why…

1. The Yellow Pages Are No Longer Effective.

The Yellow Pages used to be the #1 place consumers looked when they needed an inspector. In today's market, very few people still reference the printed Yellow Pages. In fact, much of the new generation has never been exposed to the Yellow Pages, and only knows of the Internet as a way to search for local businesses.

2. Search Engines & Social Media is What's Being Used.

Instead, this generation now looks to search engines like Google, Yahoo, Bing, and social media sites like Facebook and

Twitter, to which they ask for referrals from their friends and family.

- A new survey of 2,000 consumers found that 86 percent of those surveyed used the Internet to find a local business. And if your home inspection business isn't showing up – you're in BIG trouble!

- 74 percent of the respondents said they use a search engine when they are looking for a local retail or service business.

If you're not showing up on page one of Google, Yahoo and Bing for home inspection related keywords in your area, then you're missing out on a major opportunity to grow your home inspection business.

In this guide, I will show you how to ensure you put your best foot forward and show up in as many local inspection related searches in your area as possible – including neighboring cities as well!

Understanding How Search Engines Work

O ver the past ten years, the way search engines work has changed significantly; especially with the introduction of the Google map listings (Google My Business).

A majority of the home inspectors we talk with are confused about how the search engines work, and the differences between the map listings, organic listings and the (paid) pay-per-click listings.

In this section, I wanted to take a few minutes to DEMISTIFY the search engines and break down the anatomy of the search engine results page (also known as SERPs). By understanding how each component works, you can formulate a strategy to maximize the results of each.

There are 3 core components of the search engines results page:

1. Paid / Pay Per Click Listings (PPC)
2. Map Listings
3. Organic Listings

Understanding Pay Per Click Advertising

In the paid section of the search engines, you're able to choose the keywords that are relevant to your inspection business, and then you pay to be listed in this area.

So for example, if you do a Google search for 'Jacksonville Home Inspector', you'll be presented with the Pay-Per-Click listings, Map Listings and Organic listings... I've highlighted the Pay Per Click listings in the screenshot below:

The reason it's referred to as Pay-Per-Click (or PPC), is because rather than paying a flat monthly or daily fee for placement, you simply pay each time someone clicks on your ad after doing a search. Remember, your ad only shows up when someone does a search for the keywords you choice during the setup.

Like an auction, the Pay-Per-Click platform is based on a bidding system. The company that bids the highest gets the best placement. PPC is still a great way to market your business online, but should be thought of as a short-term marketing solution. PPC can get very expensive very fast, with some keywords costing as much as $10.00 per click.

However, it's a very profitable strategy to use when you know what you're doing. While SEO can take months to benefit from, pay per click advertising can get local and targeted traffic to your website in as little as 15-minutes of setting up your account.

As I mentioned a moment ago, with pay-per-click advertising, you get to choose the city and keywords you show up for.

The idea is that if someone is doing a search for 'Jacksonville Home Inspector', it's highly likely they're in need of a local inspector – and if they see your listing, they can click on it and be directed to your website.

Understanding Map Listings

The map listings have become very important because it is the first thing that comes up in the search results for most locally based searches. If someone searches **"home inspection + your city"** or **"your city + home inspection"**, chances are that the map listings will be the first thing they look at (see example below).

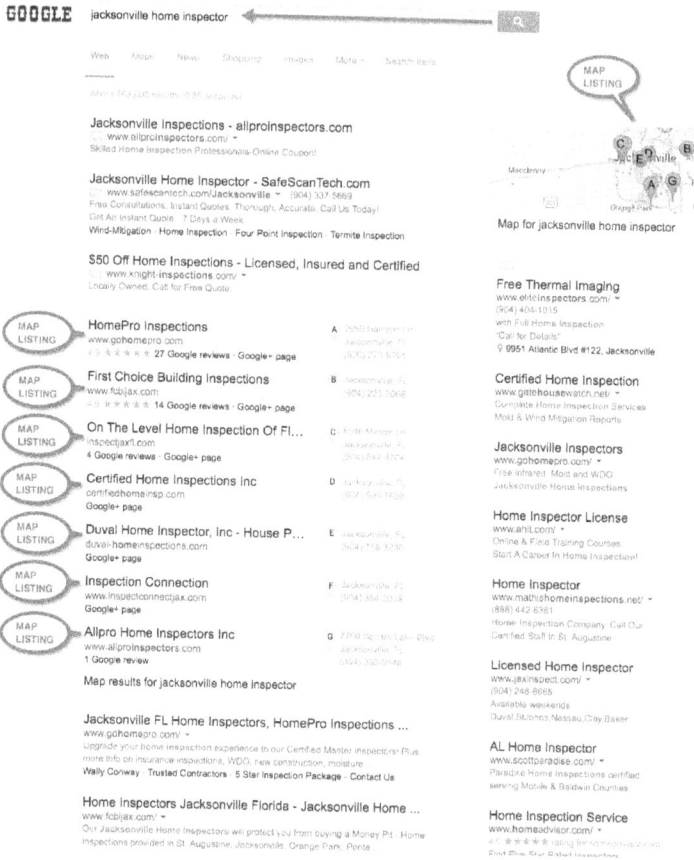

Unlike the pay-per-click section of the search engine, you can't buy your way into the map listing area -- you have to earn it. Later on in this guide, I will share our Google My Business optimization strategy. This shows you exactly what needs to be done to obtain page one placement in the map section of the search engine results.

Organic Listings (Free Natural Ranking)

The organic / natural section of the search engine results page appears directly beneath the map listings in many local searches, but appears directly beneath the paid listings in the absence of the map listings.

Look at the screenshot below to see where the 'organic listings appear'.

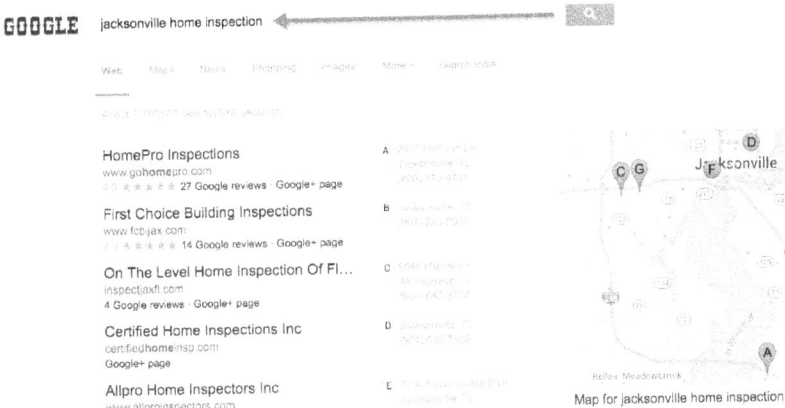

Similar to the map listings, you can't buy your way into this section of the search engines, and there's no pay per click cost associated with it. It's FREE. Later on, I will also share our search engine optimization strategy for getting ranked in this area of the search engines.

Now that you understand the 3 major components of the search engine results, and the differences between the paid listings, map listings and the organic listings, you might wonder which section is the most important?

The fact is, all three components are important and each should have a place in your online marketing strategy.

At the end of the day, you'll want to show up as often as possible when someone is searching for a home inspection in your area.

With that said, assuming you're operating on a limited budget and need to make each marketing dollar count, you should focus your investment on the sections that are going to drive the strongest return on investment.

Research indicates a vast majority of the population will glance right over the paid listings section altogether, and will instead look directly at the organic and map listings area when conducting a search.

(See heat map)

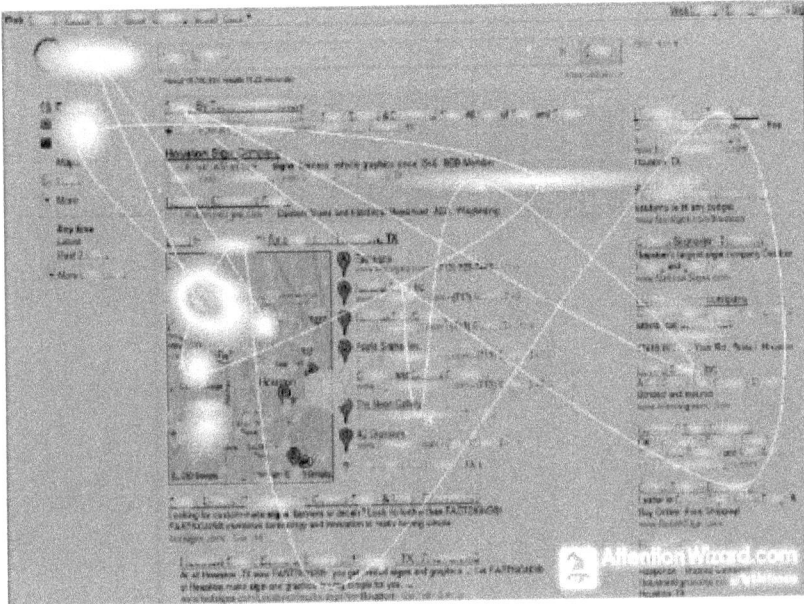

This heat map indicates where the searcher tends to view as they come onto a search engine results page.

72% of the clicks happen on the Map Listings, and within the Organic Listings as well.

28% of the clicks fall on the Pay Per Click areas. This is the section where the listings have been paid for by the advertisers through Google's AdWords program (Yahoo and Bing too).

So if you're operating on a limited budget, and need to get the best bang for your buck, you should start by focusing your efforts on the area that gets the most clicks at the lowest cost.

We have found that placement in the organic and map section of the search engines drive a SIGNIFICANTLY better return on investment than Pay-Per-Click marketing.

So how can you get your home inspection company listed in the organic and map listings? That's what we're going to be covering in the following sections.

GETTING YOUR HOME INSPECTION BUSINESS INTO THE GOOGLE MAPS LISTING

Let's Get Your Home Inspection Biz Listed in the Map Listings

If you're trying to get an idea of how to get your company listed on the Google Map, this is a great place to start. I am going to cover the core fundamentals of what the Google Map is, how it works, and what you need to do to at least get the ball rolling in the right direction towards getting your business placed.

This section of the Google search engine used to be called Google Places, Google Plus Local and Google Maps. Now it's called 'Google My Business' – and that's what we'll call it from now on…

Fundamentally, the Google My Business listing is what shows up when you type in your city + your services on Google.

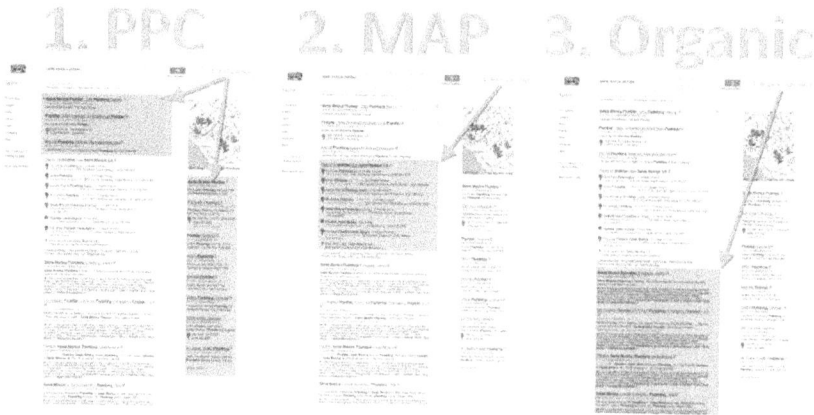

So, what do you need to do in order to make sure that you are listed on that map, and more importantly, what do you need to do to make sure you're showing up on page one over time?

To get the process started, you should go to the following Google My Business website at:

https://www.google.com/business/

Google has set up this website for business owners to tangibly claim their Google My Business listing. The latest statistics indicate that more than 89 percent of businesses have NOT claimed their Google My Business listing. This creates a great opportunity for you to beat your competition to the punch.

One of the first things you want to do is go claim your listing so you can ensure it's got all of your right information. Your phone number, your website address (if you have one), description of what you do, some pictures, maybe some coupons. More than anything else, make sure you have control of your own business listing on Google.

Some things to be aware of as you claim your Google listing.

If you have a Gmail account or some type of Google account, Google will recognize it and let you use that to claim your listing. If you don't, you're going to need to go through the process of establishing your Google account.

Once you have logged in, you will need to type in your phone number and company name. Then, the system will search the Google My Business directory to see if you're already in the database. In most cases, if you have been in business for any period of time, you're typically going to show up on the list already.

If that's the case, Google will pull up your existing listing and ask you to confirm it's yours. If you don't, there is another process that will let you add yourself to Google My Business. So if you're a new business, or if for some reason you don't already exist in the directory, you will need to press the "add new listing."

In either event, it's going to walk you through the process step-by-step…

Next, you're going to type in your company name, address, and phone number. You're going to make sure all of that information is correct.

Make sure you use your actual company name. So if you're, "Keen Eye Inspections," make sure you name it, "Keen Eye Inspections," and **not** some other facsimile thereof like "Keen Eye Inspections Jacksonville" or "#1 Inspector Keen Eye Inspections."

Don't add additional key words in that name. It's against Google's rules and policies.

It is important that you establish your NAP (Name, Address, Phone Number Profile) and that it's consistently referenced the same way across the web. Make sure that it's showing your company name, phone number, and address the same way every time.

As a starting point, if you're getting started with Google My Business, make sure you make it very simple. And make sure you use the same methodology for naming yourself across the board. The same applies with your address. If you're at 105 SW 10th Street, Suite 105, use the same exact wording everywhere. If you're going to use SW, then make sure to use SW everywhere.

If you're going to spell out Southwest, spell out Southwest. If you're going to use your suite number, use it the same everywhere: "Suite 105". Make sure you either list it, or you don't list it, and decide whether it's going to be the "unit number" or the "suite number". List it the same way EVERY single time.

Once you've added the fundamentals, make sure you add your website address to all of your listings. List it the same well – everywhere! This is very important. If you don't have a website, I definitely recommend getting on designed – we can help with you with this. On my website at www.InspectMania.com, I've shared some ideas about what the best website formats are, and what pages you must have on your website from an SEO perspective.

But make sure you add your website address to your listing. It's obviously going to drive links to your website, but it's also going to make it easier for your customers to get to you when they do find you on the Google map, or any of the other online directories.

In your description, I always encourage trying to make sure you list your services and your geographic market in the description. E.G. "Keen Eye Inspections is your full service Dallas Home Inspector (or Home Inspection Company). We provide home inspections for new home buyers, blah, blah, blah…" You get approximately 250 characters for the description area, so you really want to try and maximize that space to its fullest capability.

Directly below that, you have categories. You want to choose the categories that most specifically match what your business does. Don't add yourself to categories that aren't relevant. You can add five categories.

You do have the option to create custom categories. But always exercise the option to choose from one of the existing category as much as possible, as opposed to creating a unique category name.

The next thing you'll see is the ability to upload photos and videos. I encourage you to upload as much content here as possible. Google is looking for a complete profile and the more information you have in there, the more complete your profile appears.

You can upload up to ten pictures & five videos. Try and use real pictures. Always upload either your logo, or a picture of you in front of your truck, or a picture of you at a recent inspection. This way you're putting something up that's representative of your company and not just some stock photo. People like to know they're doing business with a person – and not an emotionless website.

Try and upload pictures that are representative of your organization. So your logo, pictures of your team, etc. This helps people quickly look at who you are and get a grasp. My preference would be logo first, and then photo second.

If you're members of your local chamber of commerce, members of the BBB, or members of an inspection association, these are the types of photos/symbols you'll want to include in your Google profile.

Save these images with keyword specific naming. So, if your first image is your logo, call it "your company name – your city service". If you're Keen Eye Inspections in Dallas, you might want to name that first image "Keen Eye Inspections – Your Dallas Home Inspector".

VIDEOS. You can upload up to five videos. The videos connect from YouTube and you don't want to miss out on this opportunity. Google owns YouTube and you should upload all five videos here. Remember to fill out EVERYTHING within your profile – many inspectors leave multiple fields blank. You don't want to do that – this is your opportunity to get that extra advantage over those inspectors that are not maximizing these opportunities.

Creating your own videos can be fun and easy… You don't have to go out and buy high-end recording equipment. Break out your android cell or the iPhone and start recording.

Shoot a video of yourself explaining who you are and what you do, and what makes you unique.

For example… "Keen Eye Inspections is a full service home inspection company, servicing the Dallas market. We do this, that and the other, we provide this, that and the other, blah, blah, blah…. Anything, anywhere, 24 hours, and seven days a week, whatever – we do it all! And as a special incentive, if you reference this video you can save 50 dollars off your inspection…"

When you're out inspecting, and you come across a major issue, pull out your cell-phone, point and start talking. This is a great time to educate the viewer on what they're looking at. This helps in establishing and positioning you as 'the expert'. The more of these type videos you can make, the better…

Not only will it help position you as an expert – it can also help in your SEO rankings. Google is known for ranking videos in their search engines too… This is another way to get your content and services out to the local public.

So make sure you leverage the five video spots Google gives you on your Google My Business profile. Adding those videos is going to help build out your Google profile, which also improves your probability of showing up on the map list as well – remember that 72% of searchers click in the map and organic listings area.

Video is also going to help people resonate with your organization. If they can feel like they know, like, and trust you, it improves the probability of you getting that call and getting that piece of business.

So right now, go upload five videos to YouTube and then connect them to your Google My Business page. The ideal scenario is to include ten pictures, and five videos – NO EXCEPTION.

If you haven't done your first inspection yet, go and inspect your own home. Reach out to a neighbor or relative and inspect their home. You want the videos and photos for your profile page.

SERVICE AREA. You can select your Service Area based on your location and miles included in your service area. Try to make this a legitimate representation of your true service area (don't over do it).

The last field on the Google My Business listing is additional information. Here, you'll essentially find just two fields. One on the left side. The other one on the right. It basically allows you type in whatever you want.

In many cases, people will get to this section and press the submit button -- feeling like they're done.

This is the area where you can really add a lot of valuable content, along with specific information about who you are and what you do, and the specific services you offer.

Then in the areas serviced section, you can type in all of the cities you service. This section gives you the ability to add some additional keyword rich information into your Google My Business listing to enhance the probability of showing up for additional key words.

Once you've got all of those things filled in, and you feel comfortable that you've got the right images, the right description, and the right content listed, then go to the next step and press "Submit."

After you 'submit', this is where the verification process takes place.

Google gives you two options for verifying your listing. Depending on if it's a new listing, sometimes Google won't offer the phone verification process.

Typically, you'll have the choice to verify via the phone or the mail. If you do have the option to choose, select the phone verification. It's instantaneous and you don't have to wait. Simply select the verify via phone option and you'll get a message indicating that Google will be calling with a PIN #.

As soon as you select the phone verification option, your telephone will practically start to ring immediately. It'll be an automated system that calls with a message similar to, "this is Google -- your pin number is 43625".

You'll then type that pin number to verify your listing. At this point, you have now officially claimed and verified your Google listing.

If for whatever reason you don't get the option to verify via phone, then you'll need to verify via the mail.

Google will send you a postcard via mail and it'll have a pin code just like the phone option. It takes a little bit longer this way, but once you get your pin number, you'll be able to log back in to verify your account.

Once you verify your Google listing, you'll the ability to log back into your Google My Business account to post status updates, add coupons, promote special offers, etc.

So fundamentally, this is where you want to start. You want to go and build out your profile as I have described. This gives you a placeholder and a higher probability of showing up on the Google map.

I wish I could tell you it's just as easy as this, and that you're going to be on page one for your city. But unfortunately, it's not that simple.

There are hundreds of businesses in your area, if not thousands; all doing the same type of thing, and many have already claimed their Google listing. So at this point, it really doesn't give you a free pass to the front of the line. But it does get you on the list.

The next step in getting placed on the map is obtaining a consistent name, address, and citation profiles across the web, and getting online reviews from legitimate users. Earlier, we talked about the fact that when you claim your Google listing, you want to use the same name, address, and phone number across the board.

Now you want to make sure you get yourself on other important online directories too. Google looks across the web and it says, "Okay, Keen Eye Inspections, in Dallas has a Google listing, but where else are they listed at online?"

Google will pull data from a variety of different places. They look at Yahoo Local. They look at Bing Local. They look at CitySearch. They look at Angie's List. They look at YP.com. They might look at Dex. They look at Merchant Circle. And the list goes on and on.

In order to improve your probability of getting a good placement on the Map listing, you need to make sure you're showing up in all of these different places with a consistent name, address, phone number, and profile. Google pulls this data to help verify if you're credible – or not.

How Reviews Will Affect Your Business Online

To improve the probability of showing up on the Google map listing, you'll need to get real reviews from actual customers online. Not just on Google, but you also need to have real reviews on the other major directories too. Directories like Yelp, Bing, Yahoo Local can play a very significant role on how well you place on Google Maps (Google My Business listings). You'll notice the companies showing up on spots A-F on page one have a tendency to have a large quantity of reviews.

When getting your reviews together, I need to point out that you don't want to try and game the system on reviews. It might be easy to think, "I'll just go out and set up a bunch of accounts and I will write up a bunch of reviews, and I'll have 55 reviews on my account."

It ain't that simple.

Google has algorithms in place to prevent people from gaming their system. In order to write a review on Google, you have to have a Gmail, or a Google account.

Google knows the historic profile of those that have Google accounts. They watch their search trends. They have IP information, which gives them information about where they are located. So Google has a pretty good idea who the legitimate users are. They have data on just about everybody. If you try to game the system, you will get caught and Google will penalize you – and will likely outright ban you.

You need to make sure you have a process in place within your business to solicit reviews from legitimate people who have used your services.

We've put together our own review acquisition system for our members to help automate the process of getting reviews from their clients after the inspection. This is important because the more reviews you can get posted online, the better it'll help with your 'expert-positioning' and rankings.

SEO STRATEGY FOR HOME INSPECTORS

Search Engine Optimization (also called SEO), is the process of getting your website to show up in the Organic (FREE / Non-PPC) section of the search engines.

There are specific things you can do both on and off your website to ensure you show up when someone types "Home Inspector + Your City" into Google, Yahoo or Bing.

In all of our years working with clients in some of the most competitive markets in the United States, we have developed a proven strategy that consistently gets our clients to the top of the search engines.

Step 1 – Build out your website and obtain more place holders on the major search engines.

A typical inspector website has only 5-6 pages (Home – About Us – Our Services – Schedule Now – Contact Us).

Unfortunately, that doesn't create a lot of indexation, or place-holders on the major search engines.

Most inspectors provide a wide variety of services including mold testing, radon testing, infrared thermal scans, new construction inspection, sellers inspection, 11-month warranty inspection, and the list goes on...

But by BUILDING out the website and creating separate pages for **EACH** of these services (combined with city modifiers), home inspectors can get listed on the search engines for each of those different keyword combinations.

Here is an example:

- Home – About – Services – Contact Us
- **Sub Pages for Each Service** – Dallas Home Inspection | Dallas 11-Month Warranty Inspection | Pre-Listing Inspection Dallas | Dallas Infrared Inspection | Dallas Commercial Inspection

Inspectors often provide services in a large number of cities outside their primary city. In order to be found on the major search engines for EACH of those sub-cities, additional pages need to be created as well:

- Sub-pages for each sub-city serviced – Atlanta Mold Testing, Marietta Mold Testing, Smyrna Mold Testing, Kennesaw Mold Testing, Vining Mold Testing, etc.
- Sub-pages for each sub-city serviced – Atlanta Radon Testing, Marietta Radon Testing, Smyrna Radon Testing, Kennesaw Radon Testing, Vining Radon Testing, etc.
- Sub-pages for each sub-city serviced – Atlanta New Construction Inspection, Marietta New Construction Inspection, Smyrna New Construction Inspection, Kennesaw New Construction Inspection, Vining New Construction Inspection, etc.

Step 2 – Optimize Pages for Search Engines:

Once the pages are built for each of your core services and sub-pages, each of the pages need to be Optimized from an SEO perspective so that the search engines understand what the page is about and list you for those words.

Here are some of the most important items that need to be taken care of for on-page search engine optimization:

- Unique Title Tag on each page
- H1 Tag re-stating that Title Tag on each Page
- Images named with primary keywords
- URL should contain page keyword
- Anchor Text on footer of each page – Atlanta Home Inspection
- XML Sitemap should be created and submitted to Google Webmaster Tools and Bing Webmaster Tools

Here's an example of a typical home inspection website title tag:

A Keen Eye Inspections

Here's an SEO Optimized Title Tag:

Atlanta Home Inspection | A Keen Eye Inspections

If you do just one thing today to start optimizing your website, make sure you work on your title tags. Make sure you DO NOT use the same title tag on each page.

Step 3 – Inbound Links

Once the pages are built out and the "on-page" SEO is complete, the next step is getting inbound links. Everything we have done to this point is laying the ground work – you have to have the pages in order to even be in the running...but it is the number of QUALITY inbound links to those pages that is going to determine placement. The only way to get your website to rank above your competition is by having MORE quality inbound links to your site.

There are a number of things you can do to increase the number of inbound links to your site.

- **Association Links** – Be sure that you have a link to your site from any industry associations you belong to (NAHI, ASHI, InterNACHI).

- **Directory Listings** – Get your site listed on as many directory type listings as possible (Angies List, Yahoo Local Directory, Judy's Book, Yelp.com, etc.).

- **Create Interesting Content / Articles** about your industry - this is probably the #1 source of inbound links because you can write an article about "How to Choose a Home Inspector" and push it out to thousands of article directory sites, each containing a link back to a specific page on your site.

If you build out your site for your services and sub-services, optimize the pages using SEO best practices and then systematically obtain inbound links to those pages and sub-pages, you will start to DOMINATE the search engines for your home inspection related keywords in your area.

SEO STRATEGY FOR HOME INSPECTORS

One of the most important components of Search Engine Optimization is Keyword Research. You need to know what people are actually searching for so you can optimize your website for keywords that will actually drive valuable traffic.

Based on our research (reviewing the historic trends on Google, Yahoo & Bing) we have developed a list of the most commonly searched keywords for the home inspection industry.

By knowing these keywords and implementing an SEO and keyword strategy with the content on your website, you can ensure you don't miss out on highly targeted traffic to your website.

You can review a listing of our top home inspection marketing keywords by clicking on the link below:

www.inspectmania.com/best-home-inspection-marketing-keywords

Directory Marketing for Home Inspectors

Ten years ago, you could place a BIG ad in the Yellow Pages and connect with a large percentage local customers when they were in need of your services.

Today, people go to a number of places online, including Google, Yahoo, Bing. But now, online directories also play a major role in how people find service providers – especially in the age of 'mobile'.

Considering that over 60% of searches are happening from mobile devices, it's in your best interest to be in as many places as you possibly can and online directories can help with that…

Take a look at the screenshot **on the next page**… When I did a search for 'San Francisco Home Inspection', five of the ten results came back from a variety of sources – the first two rankings were from Yelp.

Here are a few of the important and most searched directories you'll want to have your inspection business listed in…

- Google My Business
- Yahoo Local
- Bing Local
- YP.com

- Angies List

- CitySearch

- SuperPages

- Facebook

- Twitter

- Local.com

- FourSquare

Bay Area Home Inspections - Home Inspectors - San ... - Yelp
www.yelp.com › Home Services › Home Inspectors ▾ Yelp
★★★★★ Rating: 5 - 70 reviews
Bay Area Home Inspections - San Francisco, CA, United States. Bay Area Home
Inspections - San Francisco, CA, United States · Kat Z. Bay Area Home ...

San Francisco » Home Services » Home Inspectors - Yelp
www.yelp.com/c/sf/home_inspectors ▾ Yelp
The Best Home Inspectors in San Francisco on Yelp. Read about places like: Bay
Area Home Inspections, Vista Inspection Services, LLC, General Contractors ...

Bay Area Home Inspections - Home Inspection services for ...
bayareahomeinspections.com/ ▾
Bay Area Home Inspections provides reliable, low-cost home inspections for your
home, condo, roof, fireplace and more. San Francisco Bay Area

San Francisco/ Bay Area Home & Termite Inspection ...
www.on-siteinspections.com/ ▾
On-Site Inspections provides comprehensive narrative home inspection reports on
single family ... Our San Francisco Home and Termite Inspection Services

10 Best Home Inspection Services in San Francisco, CA
https://www.thumbtack.com/ca/san-francisco/home-inspection/ ▾ Thumbtack
Jan 7, 2015 - Here is the definitive list of San Francisco's home inspectors as rated by
the San Francisco, CA community. Want to see who made the cut?

Your San Francisco & Bay Area Home and Termite ...
www.sanfranciscohomeinspection.com/ ▾
A professionally conducted home and termite inspection by San Francisco based On-
Site Inspections, the most qualified, top rated Home Inspection and Termite ...

Home Inspection in San Francisco, San Mateo, Marin and ...
www.vistainspectionservices.com/ ▾
Home Inspection in San Francisco, Daly City, Pacifica, San Bruno, San Carlos, South
San Francisco, San Rafael, Tiburon, Burlingame, Belmont, Redwood City ...

Find BBB Accredited Home Inspectors near San Francisco, CA
www.bbb.org/...san-francisco/.../home-inspection ▾ Better Business Bureau
Find BBB Accredited Home Inspectors near San Francisco, CA - your guide to trusted
San Francisco, CA Home Inspection Service, recommended and BBB ...

San Francisco Department of Building Inspection
sfdbi.org/ ▾
Seal of the City and County of San Francisco · Department of Building Inspection. Lite
Site/Full Site. Home · Permit ... Inspection Services. Inspection Services.

San Francisco Home Inspectors Recommendations - San ...
www.angieslist.com › Local Reviews › CA › San Francisco ▾ Angie's List
... in San Francisco. Read Ratings and Reviews on San Francisco Home Inspectors
on Angie's List so you can pick the right Home Inspector the first time.

Map for san francisco home

Find Five-Star Rated Inspectors
Backed By Our 24/7 Project Suppo

The Home Inspectors
www.thehomeinspectors.biz/ ▾
Residential Inspections since 198
San Jose & greater South Bay Are

Affordable Home Inspecto
www.thumbtack.com/Home-Insp
Find Certified Home Inspectors
Compare Quotes & Save. Search N

See your ad here »

You can add your company to most of these directories for FREE of charge, and that will serve its purposes from a citation development perspective (getting your name, address and phone number more visible online).

If you have extra room in your budget, we have seen the following directories drive a solid ROI:

- Angies List
- Kudzu
- City Search
- Yelp
- Merchant Circle
- Eventective
- Thumbtack

Also, don't forget about the directories that come with your association membership... Many home inspection associations allow their members to create a listing in their online directories – make sure you check that out!

7 SOCIAL MEDIA STRATEGIES FOR INSPECTORS

There is a lot of BUZZ around Social Media (Facebook, Twitter, YouTube, Pinterest, Instagram, etc.), but how can home inspectors leverage Social Media?

How can you actually use social media to grow your inspection business?

It all starts with understanding that Social Media is the new word of mouth. The best way to use Social Media is to enhance the engagement and loyalty of your existing customers, and by extension of that, social media platforms will grow your repeat business and word of mouth business.

Here are a few things you can do yourself...

Setup social media profiles on the major social media websites for your inspection business:

- Facebook
- Twitter
- YouTube
- LinkedIn

- Google My Business
- FourSquare

If you have a database of your clients, send out an email blast letting them know you want to connect with them on social media. Offer them some incentive to "Like You", "Follow You" and / or "subscribe" to you.

- Discount off next purchase
- Discount for their friends and family
- Something of value for FREE

Add social media to your day-to-day business practices and systematically invite your customers to engage with you on-line. Add links to your business cards, brochures, marketing materials, website and email signature.

Be sure to invite all of your customers to engage after service via follow up email, or as an insert in your invoice.

POST VALUABLE CONTENT – This may be the most important component of your Social Media Strategy. If you have thousands of fans and followers, but don't add value… you will have accomplished nothing.

You need to post relevant updates, tips, ideas, techniques, news and special promotions on a consistent basis. Try to keep 90% of your posts informational and 10% (or less) promotional.

Engage with your customers – You need to stay on top of your social media profiles and engage with your fans and fol-lowers…

YOUR COMPLETE WEBSITE CHECKLIST

I've outlined a few ideas for helping you get your home inspection website ready for the search engines.

Selecting the Right Domain Name & URLs

The domain name is part of the identity of your business. The URL chosen can have a significant impact on brand identity and in a lesser extent, keyword-ranking performance.

How your website domain name and the page names you create for each of your pages can also have a significant impact on the crawl-a-bility and ranking of your web site too…

For example:

www.KeenEyeInspections.com/inspector-your-home

versus…

www.KeenEyeInspections.com/atlanta-home-inspection

It'll be more to your advantage to name your pages like the second example, versus the second example…

But even the following example could provide you with more of an advantage than the first two – see below:

www.AtlantaHomeInspection.com/pre-warranty-inspection-atlanta

Some people say that having domains with keywords in it don't matter... I disagree – I believe every little bit helps and the more factors you can drop into the equation to help you, the better...

So... Here are a few guidelines to be conscious of with regards to domain names:

__ Keep it short and memorable

__ Try to select a domain that uses keywords

__ Site.com should redirect to www.site.com

__ Home page should redirect to root

__ No underscores in filenames

__ Use keywords in directory names

__ Make sure to have multiple pages per directory

__ Register domain name for minimum of 5+ years

__ You should own multiple versions of your domain name:

- .com
- .org

- .net
- .biz

Website Logo:

The logo lends directly to brand identity and site identification. It also creates a certain element of appeal and professionalism in the mind of the visitor. It holds an important role in visitor assurance & navigation.

- Your logo should display company name clearly
- Make sure your logo isn't hidden among clutter
- Your logo should link to home page
- Try and make your logo unique and original
- Use tagline consistently across site

Design Considerations

The site design is essentially the first impression someone gets when they land on your site. You may have all your usability and SEO elements in place, but if the design is lacking, your visitor's impression of you will be lacking as well.

A visually appealing site cannot only bolster trust and credibility, but it can make you stand out among other less-appealing sites in your industry.

A few tips to consider in designing your website...

- Instant site identification
- Crisp, clean image quality

- Clean, clutter-less design
- Consistent colors and type
- Whitespace usage
- Minimal distractions
- Targets intended audience
- Meets industry best practices
- Easy to navigate
- Descriptive links
- Good on-page organization
- Easy to find phone number
- Don't link screen captures
- Skip option for flash
- Consistent page formatting
- Font size is adequate
- Font type is friendly
- Paragraphs not too wide
- Visual cues to important elements
- Good overall contrast
- Low usage of animated graphics
- Uses obvious action objects
- Avoid requiring plugins
- Minimize the use of graphics

- Understandable graphic file names
- No horizontal scrolling
- Non-busy background
- Recognizable look and feel
- Proper image / text padding
- Uses trust symbols
- Works on variety of resolutions
- Works on variety of screen widths

Architectural Issues

Website architecture can make or break the performance of a website in the search engines. Poor architectural implementation can create numerous stumbling blocks, if not outright roadblocks to the search engines as they attempt to crawl your website.

On the other hand, a well-implemented foundation can assist both visitors and search engines as they navigate through your website, therefore increasing your site's overall performance.

Here are a few things to think about when structuring your website.

- Correct robots.txt file
- Declare doctype in HTML
- Validate HTML
- Don't use frames

- Alt tag usage on images
- Custom 404 error page
- Printer friendly
- Underlined links
- Differing link text color
- Breadcrumb usage
- Nofollow cart links
- Robots.txt non-user pages
- Nofollow non-important links
- Review noindex usage
- Validate CSS
- Check broken links
- No graphics for ON/YES, etc.
- Page size less than 50K
- Flat directory structure
- Proper site hierarchy
- Unique titles on all pages
- Title reflects page info and heading
- Unique descriptions on pages
- No long-tail page descriptions
- Proper bulleted list formats
- Branded titles

- No code bloat
- Minimal use of tables
- Nav uses absolute links
- Good anchor text
- Text can be resized
- Key concepts are emphasized
- CSS less browsing
- Image-less browsing
- Summarize all tables

Navigation

A strong, user-friendly and search engine friendly navigation is essential in helping people and bots through your site. Your visitors need to find information quickly with minimal hunting and the search engines need to be able to follow the navigation to reach all site pages with the fewest number of jumps (clicks) necessary.

If the navigation is broken or doesn't get people (or search engines) where they need to go, the performance of a site will suffer.

- Located top or top-left
- Consistent throughout site
- Links to Home page
- Links to Contact Us page

- Links to About Us page
- Simple to use
- Indicates current page
- Links to all main sections
- Proper categorical divisions
- Non-clickable is obvious
- Accurate description text
- Links to Login
- Provides Logout link
- Uses Alt attribute in images
- No pop-up windows
- No new window links
- Do not rely on rollovers
- Avoid cascading menus
- Targets expert and novice users
- Absolute links

Content

Content is an essential part of the persuasion process. Pretty, image-based sites may be appealing to the eye, but it's the content that appeals to the emotional and logical centers of the brain.

The inclusion of content as well as the effectiveness of the writing is all crucially important to the sales process.

- Grabs visitor attention
- Exposes need
- Demonstrates importance
- Ties need to benefits
- Justifies and calls to action
- Gets to best stuff quickly
- Reading level is appropriate
- Customer focused
- Benefits and features
- Targets personas
- Provides reassurances
- Consistent voice
- Eliminate superfluous text
- Reduce/explain industry jargon
- No typo, spelling or grammar errors
- Contains internal contextual links
- Links out to authoritative sources
- Enhancing keyword usage (SEO)
- Date published on articles/news
- Web version of PDF docs available

- Consistent use of phrasing
- No unsubstantiated statements

Content Appearance

Great content can get lost if it's not easy to read or thrown into an otherwise cluttered page. Ensuring that your content fits visually into the site is just as important as having good content to begin with. If you want the sales message to get across, your visitors will need to read it.

Here are a few guidelines to consider...

- Use short paragraphs
- Use sub-headings
- Use bulleted lists
- Make sure to have 'call to action' on all pages
- Good contrast
- No overly small text for body
- No overly small text for headings
- Skimmable and scannable
- Keep link options in close proximity

Links and Buttons

Links and calls to action are a great way to allow visitors to navigate from page to page, finding the information they feel is important to helping them make the purchase decision.

Without these calls to action many visitors will simply not know what they are expected to do next.

- Limit the number of links on a page
- Avoid small buttons and tiny text for links
- Leave space between links and buttons
- Avoid using images as the only link
- Link important commands
- Underline all links
- Accurately reflects the page it refers

Homepage

The home page is often the single largest entry-point. It is the page that gives the visitor the sense of who you are and what they can expect. Go wrong here and it can be all over before it begins.

- No splash page
- Instant page identification
- No Flash
- Provides overview of site
- Site purpose is clear
- Robot meta: NOODP, NOYDIR

About Us Page

Studies have shown that conversion rates for visitors who have visited the About Us page increase measurably. Those who visit here are looking for a few extra elements of trust that will help them decide whether to continue on or move on. What they find can mean the difference in a conversion or the visitor leaving your site for a competitor's.

- Adequately describe company
- Show team biographies
- Show mission statement
- Up to date information
- Note associations, certifications and awards
- Links to support pages:
- Contact page
- Investor relations
- Company news
- Registration info
- Job opportunities
- Newsletters
- Link to social media profiles

Contact Us Page

Those who land on this page are showing clear intent in wanting to get in touch with you. Providing only a few ways to contact you can alienate visitors who have a particular preference.

Providing robust contact options and information ensures that you capture as many would-be customers as possible.

- Easy to find
- Multiple contact options:
- Phone
- Fax
- Email
- Form
- Chat
- Street map
- Hours of operation
- Final call to action
- Multiple points of contact:
- Customer service
- Inquiries
- General info
- Billing
- Management team
- Form requires only essential info

Services Page

The services page has a very singular focus. Its job is to provide the visitor with the information about the service they need to be convinced that it is exactly what they are looking for. If your service pages cannot convince visitors to call, then you're simply dead in the water.

- Visible calls to action
- Clear contact info (phone #)
- Consistent layout
- Clear service presentation
- Guarantee info
- Service description
- Customer reviews
- Clutter-free page
- Service Areas

Help and FAQ Pages

If your customers are digging through your help and FAQ pages, chances are they are close to making a decision to purchase and they just need a little extra bump.

- Avoid marketing hype
- Link to additional resources
- Customer support
- Q & A

Privacy and Security Pages

While most visitors won't read Privacy and Security pages, they do provide necessary assurances that visitors look for in terms of being able to trust you. However, when visitors do click into these pages, certain information needs to be presented to them to ensure their needs are met.

- Present info in easy to read format
- Provide section summaries
- Identify information types collected
- Explain how cookies are used
- Explain how user information will be used
- Explain how info will be protected
- Link to these pages in footer
- Provide links to contact info

Sitemap

Site maps provide a one-click path to any destination within the site and a way for the search engines to quickly find and index all site pages.

Ensuring that your site maps function properly is an important part in ensuring your visitors can find what they want quickly and all site pages get properly indexed.

- Keep information current
- Link to site map in footer

- Linked from help and 404 pages
- Provide overview paragraph
- Provide intro to main sections
- Visible site hierarchy
- Descriptive text and links
- Link to xml sitemap in robots.txt file

Your Complete Internet Marketing Checklist

Here are a few things for you to be conscious of as it relates to 'off-page' search engine optimization. This is the stuff that'll help ensure you the highest possible ranking.

Setup Your Company Website:

____ Build out a page on your site for each of the services that you offer, combined with your primary city and the sub cities you service

____ Optimize the website from an SEO perspective

____ Update the Title Tag on each page (Your City + Service) sub-pages (Your City + Service), etc.

____ Update H1 Tag on each page to re-emphasize the key-word for that specific page

____ Validate your HTML code so it is "spider" compliant (http://validator.w3.org/)

____ Text link navigation at the bottom of the page. Use your keywords as anchor text.

____ Your description tag needs to work hand-in-hand with the Title to get the searcher to "click" on the listing

____ Every page should have a unique (60% of the words completely original) Title & Description

____ Add ALT tags to your main graphics and do not attempt to fool the Seacrh Engines here. Place your keyword phrase in the following areas:

____ Title Tag

____ Meta Description

____ H1 tag to begin the content

____ First paragraph of content

____ Appearing in Bold or Italic in the first three paragraphs of content (if possible, not that big of a deal)

____ Appearing in the filename (or directory name)

____ Used in anchor text to either an internal page or relevant external site.

____ Fix bad links and create XML Sitemap and submit to Google & Bing

____ Install Google Analytics for Tracking

Claim Your Local Listings on:

___ Google

___ Yahoo

___ Bing

___ City Search

___ Angie's List

___ Kudzu

___ Judies Book

___ Best of the Web

___ Hot Frog

___ Merchant Circle

___ Yelp

Setup Your Social Media Profiles:

___ Facebook

___ Twitter

___ YouTube

___ Google Plus

___ LinkedIn

Ongoing Stuff You Should Consistently Be Doing:

____ Post to your blog at least once per week with tips or industry information

____ Take that post and syndicate it to at least 5-10 online directory sites with appropriate link / anchor text pointing back to your site.

____ Post to your Social Media Profiles at least 2x per week with tips or company information.

____ Add at least 2 citations per week

____ Add at least 2 inbound links per week

Your Next Steps

Through the course of this guide, we've covered a lot of information and have taken you step-by-step through how to claim and optimize your Google Map Listing, how to optimize your website for the most commonly searched keywords in your area, how to leverage social media to get more repeat and referral business.

If you have taken action and followed our instructions, you should be well on your way to dominating the Search Engines for related keywords in your area.

Need more help?

If you've gotten to this point and feel like you need some extra help to implement some of these ideas, we are here to support you. As experts in helping home inspectors across the nation, we have had tremendous success implementing these strategies.

Request A Free Custom Online Marketing Evaluation Now

www.InspectMania.com